ALL ABOUT FALL

Scarecrows

by Calvin Harris

Consulting Editor: Gail Saunders-Smith, PhD

Capstone
press

Mankato, Minnesota

Pebble Plus is published by Capstone Press,
151 Good Counsel Drive, P.O. Box 669, Mankato, Minnesota 56002.
www.capstonepress.com

1 2 3 4 5 6 12 11 10 09 08 07

Library of Congress Cataloging-in-Publication Data
Harris, Calvin, 1980–
    Scarecrows / by Calvin Harris.
    p. cm. —(Pebble plus. All about fall)
    Summary: "Simple text and photographs present scarecrows in fall"—Provided by publisher.
    Includes bibliographical references and index.
    ISBN-13: 978-1-4296-0027-9 (hardcover)
    ISBN-10: 1-4296-0027-6 (hardcover)
    1. Scarecrows—Juvenile literature. I. Title. II. Series.
SB995.25.H37 2008
632'.68—dc22
                                                  2006102057

Editorial Credits
Sarah L. Schuette, editor; Veronica Bianchini, designer

Photo Credits
Capstone Press/Karon Dubke, 1, 5, 9, 11, 13, 15, 17, 19, 21
Corbis/Michael Boys, 7
Dreamstime/Ken Cole, cover

Pebble Plus thanks Emma Krumbee's in Belle Plaine, Minnesota, and the Minnesota Landscape Arboretum in Chaska,
    Minnesota, for the use of their locations during photo shoots.

Note to Parents and Teachers

The All about Fall set supports national science standards related to changes during
the seasons. This book describes and illustrates scarecrows in fall. The images support
early readers in understanding the text. The repetition of words and phrases helps early
readers learn new words. This book also introduces early readers to subject-specific
vocabulary words, which are defined in the Glossary section. Early readers may need
assistance to read some words and to use the Table of Contents, Glossary, Read More,
Internet Sites, and Index sections of the book.

Table of Contents

Fall Is Here 4
Scarecrow Parts 8
Fun with Scarecrows 14
Other Signs of Fall 20

Glossary 22
Read More 23
Internet Sites 23
Index 24

Fall Is Here

It's fall.

The weather is getting cooler.

Scarecrows stand

in the cornfields.

Scarecrows guard fields
and gardens.
They scare birds away
from plants and crops.

6

Scarecrow Parts

Scarecrows look like people. They wear shirts and pants stuffed with yellow straw.

Scarecrows wear boots

on their straw feet.

Scarecrows wear hats
on their orange
pumpkin heads.

Fun with Scarecrows

People use scarecrows
as fun fall decorations.

14

People dress scarecrows

in funny ways.

People wear scarecrow

costumes on Halloween.

Other Signs of Fall

Scarecrows are a sign of fall.
What are other signs
that it's fall?

Glossary

decoration—an object that makes a place or another object prettier or more exciting

field—an area of land where crops grow

guard—to protect or keep watch over a person or a place

Halloween—a fall holiday where people dress up in costumes and go out trick-or-treating

straw—the dried stalks of field crops; straw usually has a yellow color.

weather—the conditions outside at a certain time and place

Read More

Latta, Sara L. *What Happens in Fall?* I Like the Seasons! Berkeley Heights, N.J.: Enslow Elementary, 2006.

Moulton, Mark Kimball. *Scarecrow Pete.* Nashville: Ideals Press, 2005.

Internet Sites

FactHound offers a safe, fun way to find Internet sites related to this book. All of the sites on FactHound have been researched by our staff.

Here's how:

1. Visit *www.facthound.com*

2. Choose your grade level.

3. Type in this book ID **1429600276** for age-appropriate sites. You may also browse subjects by clicking on letters, or by clicking on pictures and words.

4. Click on the **Fetch It** button.

FactHound will fetch the best sites for you!

Index

clothing, 8, 10, 12, 16

costumes, 18

decorations, 14

fall, 4, 14, 20

fields, 4, 6

gardens, 6

guarding, 6

Halloween, 18

pumpkin heads, 12

scaring, 6

straw, 8, 10

weather, 4

Word Count: 85
Grade: 1
Early-Intervention Level: 12